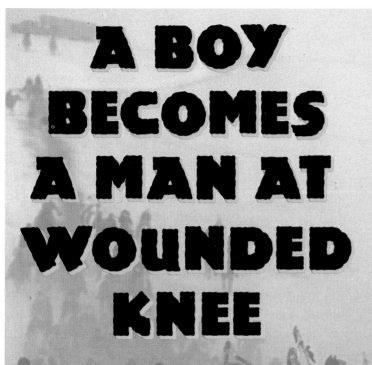

A BOY
BECOMES
A MAN AT
WOUNDED
KNEE

A BOY BECOMES A MAN AT WOUNDED KNEE

Ted Wood
with
Wanbli Numpa Afraid of Hawk

WALKER AND COMPANY   NEW YORK

To the children
of the Lakota Nation

Copyright © 1992 by Ted Wood
All rights reserved. No part of this book may be reproduced or transmitted
in any form or by any means, electronic or mechanical, including
photocopying, recording, or by any information storage and retrieval
system, without permission in writing from the Publisher.
First published in the United States of America in 1992
by Walker Publishing Company, Inc.
Published simultaneously in Canada by Thomas Allen & Son
Canada, Limited, Markham, Ontario
Library of Congress Cataloging-in-Publication Data
Wood, Ted, 1965-
  A boy becomes a man at Wounded Knee / Ted Wood with Wanbli Numpa
Afraid of Hawk.
    p. cm.
Summary: Describes the events that led to the massacre of Lakota (Sioux)
Indians at Wounded Knee in 1890 and the experiences of a young boy as he
rides with his people to commemorate this event one hundred years later.
  ISBN 0-8027-8174-8 (Cloth). –ISBN 0-8027-8175-6 (Rein)
  1. Dakota Indians–Juvenile literature. 2. Wounded Knee Creek, Battle of,
1890–Anniversaries, etc.–Juvenile literature. 3. Wanbli Numpa Afraid of
Hawk–Juvenile literature. [1. Dakota Indians. 2. Indians of North America.
3. Wanbli Numpa Afraid of Hawk. 4. Wounded Knee Creek, Battle of, 1890.]
I. Wanbli Numpa Afraid of Hawk. II. Title
E99.D1W93 1992
973.8'6–dc20   92-1218
                      CIP
                      AC
Book design, map, and calligraphy by Georg Brewer
Printed in the United States of America
10 9 8 7 6 5 4 3 2 1

Contents

Introduction

By mid-1890, the Indian wars in the American West were over. The great buffalo herds that fed the Plains Indians had been wiped out by government hunters, and white settlers streamed into Indian territory looking for gold and ranchland. Facing starvation and loss of their hunting grounds, the once proud tribes were forced onto government reservations where there was food but no more freedom. The Indians would never again roam and hunt openly on the plains.

But one great tribe resisted the move from its traditional land—the mighty Lakota (Sioux) Nation, the largest of the plains tribes. The nation was made up of many bands that spread from Wyoming to North Dakota, and its people were famed horsemen and warriors. In 1876, the bands had come together at the Little Bighorn River in Montana to wipe out Colonel George Custer and the Seventh Cavalry. The Battle of Little Bighorn was the worst defeat ever suffered by the U.S. Cavalry.

For fourteen years after, soldiers swarmed the plains,

chasing the Lakota war chiefs who had beaten Custer. Crazy Horse, chief of the Oglala Lakota, hid from the soldiers for more than a year before surrendering with his starving people at Fort Robinson, Nebraska, in 1877. There a soldier stabbed Crazy Horse in the back and killed him.

Sitting Bull, the great chief of the Hunkpapa Lakota, escaped to Canada with his band. To bring him back, the U.S. government offered Sitting Bull a pardon. But when Sitting Bull returned, the promise was broken. On December 15, 1890, police surrounded Sitting Bull's little cabin on the Standing Rock reservation in North Dakota. They came to arrest the proud war chief, but instead, they shot Sitting Bull as he prepared to surrender.

Another Lakota chief, Big Foot, was camped on the Cheyenne River sixty miles away. When word of Sitting Bull's death reached him, he was scared. Big Foot was now the main chief and he feared that the Seventh Cavalry, Custer's old brigade, would attack his small band next. Where could they go, Big Foot wondered? They had no food—only a few horses—and it was bitter cold.

On December 18, Big Foot started his band south to Pine Ridge, South Dakota, where the Oglala chief Red Cloud could protect them. Without food, the 150-mile journey seemed impossible, but they had no choice. With only a few horses to carry their supplies, the people pulled tepees, children, and elders on tree branches behind them. For five days, with temperatures forty degrees below zero, the starving band crossed the windswept Badlands, always fearing the enemy coming behind.

Forty miles from Pine Ridge, the band ran into a cavalry patrol. Chief Big Foot was dying of pneumonia, and he was being carried in a wagon. He raised himself up from his bloodstained blankets and put a white flag of truce on the wagon. The soldiers quickly moved Big Foot to an army ambulance and took the rest of the band to the cavalry camp at Wounded Knee Creek, where they were ordered to spend the night. All 350 Lakota were freezing and starving, but they were almost home.

During the night, the rest of the Seventh Cavalry caught up with Big Foot's band. Positioning themselves on ridges above Wounded Knee Creek, the soldiers surrounded the Indians, pointing their guns and cannons on the camp. The next morning, December 29, the commander went to Big Foot's tepee and told him to put all the weapons in camp in a big pile. Big Foot agreed. He had nothing to fear, he thought, since his people were showing the white truce flag.

The soldiers went tepee to tepee, taking everything from knives to rifles. They piled the weapons in the center of the camp. Suddenly, a gunshot was heard. No one knows where it came from, but within seconds the soldiers on the ridge opened fire on the camp. The Indians were helpless. Bullets and cannon shells rained down on everyone. Women tried to escape with their children, but they were killed. Within minutes it was over. Nothing moved in camp. More than three hundred men, women, and children, including Big Foot, lay dead. Only about fifty Lakota escaped.

The Seventh Cavalry received twenty-seven medals of honor for killing Big Foot's helpless people in what was called a "battle" that morning at Wounded Knee. For the Lakota, it was a massacre that tore open the heart of the Indian people for the next hundred years. The government never apologized and the dead were never honored properly. The wound never healed.

But in 1990, a group of brave Lakota horsemen went on a journey to heal the Lakota nation and bring the suffering of the massacre to an end. An eight-year-old Lakota boy rode too, on a trip that would teach him his past and make him a man from then on. This is his story.

1 Mending the Sacred Hoop

*A people's dream died at Wounded Knee. The
nation's hoop is broken and scattered. There is no
center any longer, and the sacred tree is dead.*
—Black Elk, Oglala medicine man

My name is Wanbli Numpa Afraid of Hawk. I am an Oglala
Lakota and in the old language my name means Two
Eagles. I live with my family on the Cheyenne River
Reservation in South Dakota, near Cherry Creek. Our
house is only a few miles from the Cheyenne River, where
Big Foot and his people lived.

My dad, Rocke, and my *lala* (grandfather) started telling
me about Big Foot and his walk to Wounded Knee five
years ago, when I was four years old. They told me that
my great-*lala* was with Big Foot at Wounded Knee. He was
only ten years old, almost my age. When the soldiers
started shooting, he hid in a creek gully, my dad said.
Bullets were flying everywhere, but he didn't get shot.

This is my great-great-grandfather, Afraid of Hawk. We're not sure if he was at the Wounded Knee massacre, but his son was one of the few survivors that day.

Then, he ran up the creek and escaped into the hills.

At first he hid from the soldiers. He was alone and frightened. Then he walked for miles into the Badlands until he came to some high cliffs. There was only one way up, so he started to climb. He was still scared of the soldiers. On top, there was a big group of Lakota who had escaped too, and they took care of my great-*lala*. They stayed there a long time, until it was safe to come down. My dad told me this place is called the Stronghold, and it's very sacred to us because it protected our ancestors.

But even after all these years our people were still in pain from Wounded Knee, my dad said, and he wanted to do something to help. So five years ago, he went with my uncles, Alex White Plume and Birgil Kills Straight, to see a medicine man named Curtis Kills Ree. They asked Curtis what could be done to end the Lakota's sadness.

The medicine man told them that the massacre had broken the sacred hoop of the world. The hoop is the unity of all life for the Lakota. When our people were killed at Wounded Knee, there was such sadness that the Lakota people lost their way for one hundred years. They forgot how to be strong together as a tribe. To mend the sacred hoop, he said, my dad and uncles had to take horses and wagons on the same path Big Foot and his people traveled. They had to leave at the same time Big Foot left, travel the same way his people did, sleep in the same

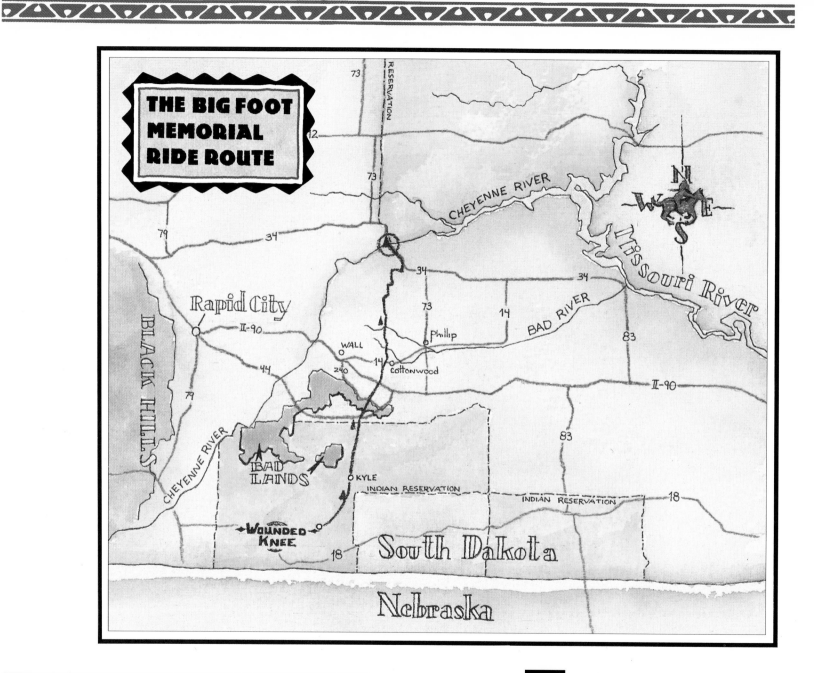

THE BIG FOOT
MEMORIAL
RIDE ROUTE

73

RESERVATION

12

73

CHEYENNE RIVER

N
W   E
S

Missouri River

79

34

34

34

Rapid City

I-90

73   14

BAD RIVER

83

BLACK HILLS

44

240   14

WALL

Phillip

Cottonwood

79

I-90

CHEYENNE RIVER

83

BAD
LANDS

KYLE

INDIAN RESERVATION

INDIAN RESERVATION

18

WOUNDED
KNEE

18

South Dakota

Nebraska

places, and feel the same cold. They had to do this five times for five years. The last year would be the one hundredth anniversary of the massacre, and then the hoop would be mended. The journeys would wipe away the tears of sadness so that Lakota children, like me, could lead the Lakota as one tribe into the future.

The first four winters, I watched my dad leave with our horses for the ride. I wanted to go so much, but I was too young. It was a hard and dangerous ride. But in the winter of 1990, I was eight years old and I was strong enough to go. For four years I had prepared for this and now it was time to become a man. Three months before the ride, I told my mother and dad that I wanted to go because this was the last ride and the one hundredth anniversary, and I wanted to pray for our ancestors who died.

In the old days Lakota boys took tests to become men. They had to shoot arrows at targets, hunt bison, or steal horses from the enemy. Now, the Big Foot ride was my test and I made a sacred promise to finish the ride. My dad was very proud and so was my mother, but she was worried because I was her only boy.

I was scared too. But I thought that if my great-*lala* did it when he was a boy, so could I. My dad and I prepared three months for the ride. Every day, he helped me saddle my sister's horse, Wanbli Wiyaka (Eagle Feather), and his big horse, Red, and we rode through the hills and the cottonwood trees in the creek near our house. Wanbli Wiyaka is a black-and-white paint horse. He looks like a checkerboard. He's a good horse—he doesn't run too fast, and he's not scared of cars. He's really calm and would be good on the ride.

My dad said it was important to prepare our spirits too. The ride had many dangers because of all the suffering spirits along the trail. To protect us, he said, we needed to make our minds strong and pure. To do this we went to the sweat lodge behind our house and prayed. The sweat lodge is a sacred part of our Lakota religion. It's a small dome made of willow branches curved and stuck in the ground with a canvas cover. There's only one opening and inside there's a hole in the ground where we put hot rocks. The sweat purifies our bodies and spirits. In our culture, the lodge represents a mother's belly, and when we're inside it's like being an unborn baby. When we come out, we are reborn and pure again.

When we went inside, it was very dark and hot. My dad put water on the rocks and it got hotter and hotter. We started to sweat and took turns saying prayers for our ancestors and for the four-leggeds (horses) to be strong on the ride. After that, we left the sweat lodge and rubbed the horses' legs with sagebrush. Then we lit the sage and let the smoke carry over the horses and over us. The sacred smoke purified us and protected us.

The night before the ride, my whole family went to my school gym, where all the Big Foot riders gathered for a ceremony. The gym was full of riders from all the Lakota reservations, white people, and visitors from other countries. We all stood in a circle on the floor and when the drums and singing started we began a traditional dance. The circle moved around the gym slowly. I saw only one rider younger than I was. Everyone else looked so strong. I was excited, but I was nervous that I was too small.

When the dancing stopped, my dad and uncles led some prayers for the group, and the riders made promises to be strong, to have good thoughts on the ride, and to remember their ancestors. We danced some more and I played with my cousins, thinking about how hard the next week would be.

2 Day One: The Big Foot Memorial Ride

On December 23, we woke up early and it was really cold. This was the day the Si Tanka Wokiksuye (The Big Foot Memorial Ride) began, and even though I was excited, I was scared too. Outside it was thirty degrees below zero, and there was snow on the ground. When we went to get the horses the air was so cold it hurt to breathe. I hoped I had enough clothes and worried that my feet and hands might get too cold. Would I be able to ride 150 miles? What if I fell off my horse and broke my arm?

I got into the car with my mother and two sisters. My dad brought the horses behind in the truck. I wanted to be a man, so I didn't tell anyone I was scared. My mom was too worried anyway, so I kept quiet all the way to Bridger, the place the ride started on the Cheyenne River.

When we got to Bridger, there were people and horses everywhere. I had never seen so many riders in one place. I couldn't recognize anybody because they were wrapped in layers and layers of clothes. My mom took me inside a little building where riders were getting warm, and she

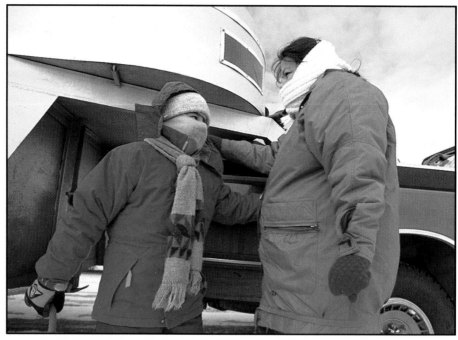

started dressing me for the ride. Soon I looked like a balloon person in all my clothes. My arms stuck straight out to the sides, and it was hard to walk. My head and face were covered in a hat that had only one hole to see through. The only things showing were my eyes.

Outside, my dad was getting our horses ready. He tied an eagle feather onto the mane of Wanbli Wiyaka to give him strength and protection, and then he tied one onto my hat. I hugged my mom good-bye and then my dad lifted me into the saddle. This was it. There was no quitting now.

We trotted off to a field where all the Big Foot riders had formed a big circle on their horses. There must have been 200 riders—all wearing feathers. Many of them were poor and didn't have much clothing. They looked cold but very strong and proud. In the center of the circle Uncle Birgil and the other leaders said prayers for the riders and their horses. Another person walked around with sacred sage smoke, purifying the horses. Suddenly everyone started hollering. Uncle Birgil broke through the circle on his horse and all the riders followed him at a gallop. It was like a river of horses and some of them went wild and

threw their riders into the snow. Wanbli Wiyaka was very calm and my dad and I galloped at the back of the pack watching the line of riders stretch out in front toward the Cheyenne River.

When we got to the river, a line of riders waited to cross the ice. No one knew how thick the ice was, so only a few riders at a time could cross. I was scared the ice was going to break and I'd fall in the freezing river. But it held for everybody, and as people waved to us from the river bridge, we disappeared into the hills.

My dad and I rode together, and my cousin was in front of us. We had thirty miles to go to the first camp, and nobody talked because it was too cold. I had to bend my head to keep the freezing wind out of my eyes. I was thinking about all of Big Foot's people, especially the kids, and how they must have been freezing. They didn't have horses like I did. They were walking, and they only had moccasins and old clothes. I felt proud to be on the same trail.

Just then, my cousin's horse bellowed. The horse fell into a hole and landed on his stomach. Luckily, my cousin stayed on. He's a good rider. What if my horse did that, I thought. There seemed to be dangers all around me.

My dad and I rode on. The leaders were really fast. We couldn't see them anymore. We rode over bare, snow-covered hills, down through the gullies where the creeks

ran, and up the hills again. I didn't want to ride fast
because it was hard to stay in the saddle. As we were
coming down one hill, another rider galloped past me. But
he got too close. My foot got caught on his horse and
twisted around in the stirrup. I screamed with pain. I
stayed on Wanbli Wiyaka, but my foot hurt badly. I kept
riding, though. I wanted to keep up with the others. I
wanted to be more of a man.

But my foot was bad. It got harder and harder for me to
ride, so my dad and I slowed down to a walk. The other
riders left us behind. The hills seemed to go on forever,
and soon it got dark and colder. There was no sound
except the wind and the crunch of the snow when Wanbli

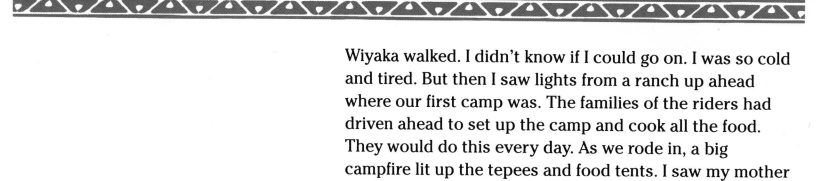

Wiyaka walked. I didn't know if I could go on. I was so cold and tired. But then I saw lights from a ranch up ahead where our first camp was. The families of the riders had driven ahead to set up the camp and cook all the food. They would do this every day. As we rode in, a big campfire lit up the tepees and food tents. I saw my mother and my sister. We had made it.

A *Wasicu* (non-Indian) farmer named McDaniels was letting the riders use his ranch, and his family was helping cold riders with their horses. They led us to a barn, where we threw our sleeping bags onto the straw. My sister and mom brought food and hot drinks. I tried to eat even though I was very tired. My foot still hurt, but I didn't say anything. I wanted to be strong. But my dad told my mom about it, and she didn't want me to go the next day. I thought about giving up, of not continuing. Then I looked around and saw riders sleeping everywhere in the barn, some with only little blankets and their heads on their saddles. They were suffering too, but they looked so proud. I wanted to be like them, a young warrior. I told my mom and dad I was going to continue. They smiled and knew it was my decision.

3 Day Two: The Ride to Big Foot Pass

The sounds of riders getting ready woke me up the next day. It was still dark, and it was colder than the day before. I didn't want to get out of my warm sleeping bag. My legs were stiff and my foot still hurt. But this day was the longest ride and I knew we needed an early start to make the thirty-six miles to the next camp.

My boots and mittens were frozen, but the more I moved the more they warmed up. My dad and *lala* gathered our horses from the pens where they had eaten

and slept in the cold. Were they suffering like we were, I wondered? Wanbli Wiyaka's breath made huge clouds of steam, but his eagle feather was still attached. He looked ready to go.

We ate just a little, had some warm drinks, and headed for the prayer circle with our horses. More riders had come during the night and today the circle was big. The

leaders in the middle said a prayer, then sang a song about the sacredness of the riders and their horses. Just as fast as before, the leaders stopped singing and took to the trail. This day, my dad and I were closer to the front. Uncle Birgil was leading, carrying the Big Foot staff. The staff is a long wooden pole with a hoop on the end. Eagle feathers are attached to the hoop. The staff is a symbol of the suffering we will feel on our sacred journey. My *lala* was next to him carrying another staff. His staff stood for our family and our ancestors.

I looked around and saw all the different people who were on the journey. There were Indians and *Wasicus*. Elders, women, and teenagers also rode, and the one boy younger than me was on a tiny white horse with a long white mane. An old Lakota woman rode in a wagon with her little grandchildren, a wagon like Big Foot had.

Some people walked too. There was a Japanese woman, a holy woman, beating a little drum as she walked. A small group walked with her, Japanese and white. There were runners too, Lakota runners who had started a week ago up at Sitting Bull's grave on the Standing Rock Reservation. They were all brave to be on foot in this terrible cold, and they gave me courage.

We stayed on small dirt roads for a while, because of all the fences on the farmland. We passed strange places with barbed wire and satellite dishes and my dad told me these

were nuclear missile silos. It made me think of other people being killed in wars. In the beginning, Uncle Birgil told us to pray for *Wolakota* (peace) and that massacres like Wounded Knee would never happen again, anywhere. When I saw the silos, I prayed.

Lots of people followed us in cars as we got near the interstate. My mom and sisters were already at the next camp helping with food for the riders. The wind blew so hard that the snow blinded us and made deep piles on the sides of the road. Once, the wagon slipped off the road and went into the deep snow. The wheels got stuck and the wagon tipped over, but the grandmother and the kids didn't get hurt.

When we got to the interstate, we crossed under a bridge along a creek and we rode onto the open, flat plains toward the Badlands and Big Foot Pass. There were no roads here, but some photographers from France followed us in their trucks. They kept racing ahead of the leaders and driving through the horses. Nobody was supposed to go ahead of the staff bearers, and it made me mad to see them breaking the rules. I hoped they wouldn't bring us bad luck.

It was really blowing out there in the open. My hands were so cold it was hard to hold on. Just then, my horse spooked and started bucking. I couldn't hold on. I flew way up in the air and came down on my arm in the snow. I

thought I had broken my arm because I couldn't move it. My dad stopped and lifted me back onto my horse. He wanted me to keep riding into camp. I didn't know if I could. But dad kept telling me I could, that I had to. It was the only way to get back.

Finally, far off on the plain, I saw the tepees. We rode fast and the horses kicked up a big cloud of snow. The camp was already prepared for the riders. There were food tents, tepees, and a big fire going. When we got there, I could hardly stay in the saddle. Another uncle lifted me out of the saddle and carried me to his truck to get warm. I couldn't move. I stayed in there a few hours and ate and got my strength back. Luckily, my arm wasn't broken. I'd be able to ride again.

In the evening after everyone ate, my mom, dad, and I went to the big campfire to listen to stories. It was so cold we all wrapped up in one blanket and got as close to the fire as we could. Some people had so many clothes on that they didn't even know it when burning embers fell on them.

We listened to funny stories that made everyone laugh. But we were all tired and frozen. And we were thinking about the next day when we would go over Big Foot Pass. The flat land where we were camped dropped right down into the Badlands. There's a big wall, like a cliff, and there's only one way down it. Big Foot took all his people

down this wall, and tomorrow we would go there.

After the stories many of the riders left camp to spend the night with their families. It was too cold for the children and they didn't have good sleeping bags. But my uncles and the leaders stayed behind with their sacred staffs to keep Big Foot's spirit in the camp. It was all right to leave, they said, because we would remember Big Foot wherever we slept. My family and I left the camp to spend the night at my auntie's house not far away.

4 Days Three and Four: Big Foot Pass to Redwater Creek

The next morning I was almost too tired to move. My feet and legs were sore and I couldn't carry my saddle out to the car. I wanted to go, but I was worried about riding through the Badlands. I wasn't strong enough. I decided to rest that day. It was okay, I didn't feel bad about it. I knew I would ride the next leg. It might have been too dangerous for me going over Big Foot Pass. If I got hurt badly I couldn't finish the ride. I had made a vow of manhood to finish and I didn't want to ruin that. It was better to rest up and be strong later. Everybody understood. I was disappointed, but I wasn't ashamed.

We stayed at my auntie's the whole day, and later we went out to greet the riders at the next camp at Redwater Creek. This camp was on the Pine Ridge reservation, home of the Oglala Lakota. It was way back in the bottom of a canyon. It looked like a good hiding place. Big Foot hid there one hundred years ago.

The riders came down the canyon with the staff bearers in the lead. The day had been good. No one was hurt

coming over Big Foot Pass. But it was even colder than the day before. When the men finished putting the horses in the pasture, everyone left to visit friends on the reservation.

But a small group of riders stayed at camp. They sat very quietly around a little campfire, wrapped in clothes. When I looked at them, they seemed to be dreaming. These were the fasters. They wanted to be close to the spirits of Big Foot and his people, so they weren't eating for four days. Big Foot's band didn't have any food either and they slept in the cold. The fasters slept in a small tent away from the other riders. They didn't go visit friends and they never left the camps. Their journey was the most dangerous. They looked like they felt all the sufferings of Big Foot's people. Tomorrow was their last day to fast, so other riders were building a sweat lodge where the hungry riders would pray at the end of their fast. I saw how strong our people could be and I felt honored to be a Lakota. I wanted to fast too, but I got too hungry.

The next day, all the riders honored the fasters for completing their vows. Then the people in Kyle, a town near the camp, fed everyone in the school gym. The fasters ate first and their plates were spilling over with food. There was a drum group in the gym, and little kids danced and played around all the sleeping bags on the floor. It felt good to rest. My ankle was getting better and I was almost ready to ride again.

Wanbli Wiyaka was out at the Redwater pasture and I was worried coyotes might scare him. When my dad went out to check him, he was gone. He had escaped from the

pasture and run north into the Badlands. My dad got on his horse and followed Wanbli Wiyaka's tracks. He looked all day. Finally, he found him, twenty miles into the Badlands. He was trying to get home to our ranch three days away. My dad and Wanbli Wiyaka didn't get any rest that day.

5 Day Five: Redwater Creek to Red Owl Springs

After breaking the prayer circle the next day, we headed for our last camp at Red Owl Springs twenty-six miles away. Everyone looked strong after the rest day, and they were excited to be nearing Wounded Knee. We rode in the hills now and the wind wasn't as strong. But each day the air got colder. It seemed like the closer we got to Wounded Knee, the more we had to suffer.

We rode through the town of Kyle, where they had fed

us. People lined the streets watching us go by, and lots more riders joined us. The band moved fast now, up and down hills covered in beautiful dry grass sticking out of the snow. The line of horses stretched out for miles ahead of me.

But finally the staff bearers stopped at the top of a high hill. When my dad and I got there we looked down on a road where lots of cars waited for us to come down. The leaders told everyone to line up along the top of the hill. There must have been 300 riders, and we looked like an army ready to charge down the hill. My dad told me this was the largest group of Lakota riders since the Battle of Little Bighorn when our people defeated Long Hair (Custer). But now we were riding for *Wolakota*, not war.

We charged down the hill past all the cars and crossed the road to our camp at Red Owl Springs. When we reached camp, we circled our horses again and said prayers of thanks that we had made it safely through another day. Everyone was excited that this was our last camp, but there was sadness too. This was Big Foot's last camp too, before he was shot.

The horses were hot and when we took off the saddles, big steam clouds rose into the air. Then we took them down to the creek and found openings in the ice where they could drink. Soon it was time for dinner. A big tent was set up down in the trees, out of the wind. That night,

Lakota men made big pots of Indian beef soup and fry
bread. There was coffee, cake, and sweet berry syrup.
Usually, the women made the food for the riders. But that
night the men were doing everything, to honor the women
for their strength and support.

My mom, dad, sisters, and I sat around a big fire with

everybody else and ate. While we ate, Uncle Birgil talked about the suffering and the honor of women in the Lakota culture and the world. He talked about Grandmother Earth too. He said the earth was suffering because we haven't taken good care of her. He said we had to respect the earth like our mothers. The earth was the very first woman, he said, the mother of us all. After Birgil spoke, every woman told a story about being a woman. Some were funny, some were sad, but all were very honorable.

Every day we rode for a different reason. The first day the riders suffered for children and orphans everywhere in the world. The next day we remembered the elderly, the keepers of the Lakota culture. The third and fourth days we honored the sick and the people whose spirits and bodies are in prison. On this day, we rode for the women.

That night, we went back to my auntie's house. I was nervous about the next day and I wanted to be strong. It was our last day, and it was also Big Foot's last day.

6 Day Six: The Ride to Wounded Knee

When we got to camp the next morning, my dad's horse was limping. His feet were frozen from chasing Wanbli Wiyaka around the Badlands. My dad decided to put me on Red because I was easy to carry. My dad rode Wanbli Wiyaka. Red is really big. He's the biggest horse we have. I was way off the ground and I didn't know if I could control him.

That morning our prayer circle had the most riders yet, almost 350. Many came from Pine Ridge to ride the last day. The date was December 28, the last day my ancestors were alive one hundred years ago. In the circle, Uncle Birgil told us we should ride for our ancestors who walked this way before. Also, we would pray for the next seven generations of Lakota so they would be united forever.

All the riders were quiet. They knew this was the day Big Foot was walking to his death. Grandmother Earth was suffering too. It was the coldest day yet and the wind

made everyone hide their faces. Someone said it was eighty degrees below zero. Each day we had suffered with the cold, but this was the worst one.

We had ridden 125 miles already. We had twenty-four to go. But this day was the hardest for me. When we left the prayer circle, Red ran off with me and I couldn't stop him. When I tried to sit, I bounced up, way out of the saddle. So I had to stand up, and my legs got really tired. He slowed down finally with the other horses, and my dad caught up to me.

Nobody talked. They thought about the ancestors. I couldn't stop thinking of Big Foot's people. I felt really sad and I felt mad at the whites for killing them. There weren't any warriors left in the band. Big Foot was really sick and spitting blood. His people were too cold to fight and they just wanted peace.

We rode through the trees and up to the ridge of Porcupine Butte. This was where the soldiers captured Big Foot's band. The ridge doesn't have trees and is the highest place on the reservation. When we got there the wind was angry. It blew so hard that the snow whipped along the ground and froze the horses' feet. Red had ice all over his legs and on his nose. His body was covered with frost. We had to stop while my dad chopped the ice off our horses' feet and noses.

I was frozen too. My fingers were numb and my legs

were cold and frosty. My face was covered in ice and I could see out of only one eye. I told my dad that my hands were freezing. I wanted to quit, but even more, I wanted to finish. He told me to pray for help. So I prayed to the wings (birds) and to the four-leggeds to make me warm. And I prayed to my ancestors. I knew if my great *lala* came over this ridge, with no food and thin clothes, I could do it too.

The prayers helped me. We came over the top of the ridge and looked down at Wounded Knee Creek. I could see hundreds of people there waiting to honor us. I felt really proud. The wind was biting me, but now I knew I could make it. We rode down the road and lots of cars followed behind us. We rode to Big Foot's grave and made

a big circle next to it. Uncle Birgil said a prayer thanking the spirits for our safety and a prayer to the ancestors who were killed.

I just wanted to get off and get warm. I was frozen in my saddle. We rode over to our car and my dad lifted me off Red and put me on the ground. But I was stiff and stuck in a saddle shape, and I rolled over in the snow. My mom came over, helped me up, and put a blanket around me. Then I got into the warm car and all my cousins came to honor me. They hugged me and smiled.

I had done it. I earned my first eagle feather as a Big Foot rider. I wasn't a kid anymore, I was a man.

7 The Wounded Knee Ceremony

On December 29, 1890, Big Foot and his people were killed at Wounded Knee. Exactly one hundred years later, the day after the ride, we went back to the grave site to honor the dead. We were all stiff and tired from the ride, but we got on our horses again for the ceremony. Hundreds of Lakota people were there to listen and watch.

The cemetery is big because Big Foot's people were put into one big hole. Uncle Birgil and Arvol Looking Horse, who is keeper of *Channumpa,* the sacred pipe, stood next to the grave while we circled it on our horses. *Channumpa* is the most sacred thing in the Lakota world. It's a long pipe made out of stone and wood. Arvol's ancestors have been the keepers of the pipe for hundreds of years. It was given to the Lakota by a spirit woman and it is the soul of our people.

Every horse that went by the graveyard gate was purified with sacred sage smoke. We surrounded the grave with our horses and watched the ceremony.

Birgil prayed with sage in the center and I could feel the suffering around me. There were women covered with blankets crying near the ancestors' graves. I saw how much everyone was hurt for the last hundred years. But I also felt very proud. I rode a difficult ride, was bucked off,

and got cold, but I hung in there. I was a Big Foot rider now, not a little kid.

When I got to school the next day, some of the kids were jealous. But I just felt proud. My teacher made me tell the class about the Big Foot ride. It is important to me to remember the past and to be a horseman. When I get older I want to tell my children and grandchildren about Wounded Knee and how we mended the sacred hoop. I will never forget the Si Tanka Wokiksuye.